SAME SCENERY, DIFFERENT LIFESTYLE

Rural Children on a Low Income

Jim Davis and Tess Ridge

The Children's Society
MAKING LIVES WORTH LIVING
A VOLUNTARY SOCIETY OF THE CHURCH OF ENGLAND
AND THE CHURCH IN WALES

First published in 1997

The Children's Society
Edward Rudolf House
Margery Street
London WC1X 0JL

A catalogue record for this book is available from
The British Library.

ISBN 1 899783 05 9

Cover photograph: modelled for The Children's Society.

Contents

Acknowledgements

The authors would like to thank Professor Jane Miller of the University of Bath for her support in guiding the research; and Alison Locke who conducted some of the interviews.

The map on page 3 is reproduced with the permission of Carfax Publishing Company, Abingdon.

CHAPTER *1*

Introduction

his report is about the experiences and perceptions of children and young people living in rural Somerset. The overall theme is one of rurality and its impact upon young lives. However, at the centre of the report is a rare opportunity to gain some insight into the lives and experiences of a group well hidden, both socially and statistically: rural children and young people on a low income.

This research was carried out by the Children's Participation Project based in Somerset. It forms the basis of a three-year programme of work that reduces the social exclusion experienced by children on a low income in West Somerset. The programme receives funding from the Rural Development Commission.

Although much has been written by youth work practitioners and researchers about young people in rural areas, rarely does the impact of low income feature as a distinctive issue. More often, the key focus is upon the limitations of services to young people in rural areas and the difficulties of accessing services that do exist. This is of course an important issue to highlight and it has been emphasised through a recent report by the National Youth Agency that concludes:

Young people who find themselves living in rural areas have fundamentally the same needs as young people living anywhere else. It is the variability of access to provision to meet those needs that creates disadvantage. (Phillips et al., 1994)

However, what needs further recognition is the additional burden placed on rural children and young people who also live on a low income. It is this combination of disadvantage that the research underpinning this report seeks to reveal.

RESEARCH AIMS

The aims of the research were:

1. to highlight the experiences of children and young people in rural areas through the medium of their own accounts and voices;
2. to explore the interlocking effects of rurality and low income, and reveal through children's voices their experiences of exclusion and marginalisation;
3. to inform the practice of The Children's Society and other agencies working with rural children and young people.

To fulfil these aims, the report poses a series of questions on issues of significance to rural children, highlighting opportunities for play and peer group association, transport and accessibility, provision of clubs and activities, and social space within communities.

The research sought to understand the lifestyles and experiences of children and young people living in rural areas, and the very particular circumstances and influences that rurality imposes upon their lives. Insight and understanding come through the medium of children's own accounts of their lives and what emerges is a view of rurality presented from their perspective and in their own words.

DEFINING RURAL

Any attempt to research rural poverty immediately encounters problems of definition and perception, both in terms of rurality and poverty. There is within the category 'rural' a variety of different and particular areas and communities that experience rurality in differing ways. As Cloke *et al.* (1995) point out, it is not possible to talk about 'rural' as a general concept: 'Rural is not a homogenous category and regional and intra-regional variations within what are recognised as "rural" areas will be significant'.

However, there are various studies and agency perspectives that help to frame our understanding of what could be considered 'rural'. One of the most comprehensive attempts to define rural areas was made by Cloke, initially in 1977 and then updated in 1986 (Cloke *et al.*, 1986). These studies of census data from 1971 and 1981 respectively have provided an index of rurality in England and Wales. In the index, five categories are described: extreme rural; intermediate rural;

intermediate non-rural; extreme non-rural; and urban. Districts within England and Wales can then be classified according to these degrees of rurality (see Figure 1 below). As is implicit in the category title, extreme rural describes those areas most affected by the manifestations of rural life, such as distance from urban settlements, patterns of migration and population density. The remaining categories reflect the diminishing degrees of rurality, ending with urban areas.

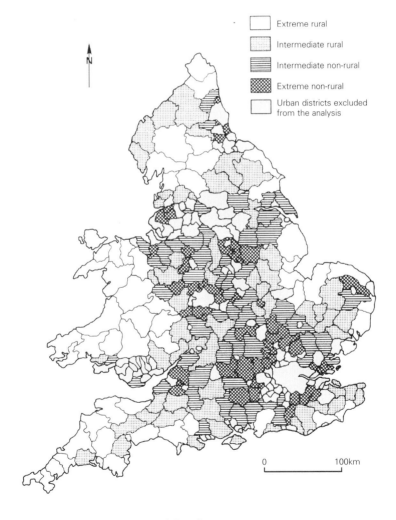

Extreme rural

Intermediate rural

Intermediate non-rural

Extreme non-rural

Urban districts excluded from the analysis

0   100km

Figure 1: The 1981B Index of Rurality

Source: *Regional Studies*, vol. 20, no. 4, p. 103

Other work focuses on types of rural communities that could be found in most of the categories described by Cloke. Derounian (1993) describes a variety of rural communities such as 'shadow' communities, which are subject to the gravitational pull of a nearby town or city, 'ghost' villages in remote areas that are active and bustling in the summer months but very much isolated and empty for much of the year, and coastal areas that have experienced the decline of the fishing industry and now rely on tourism.

However, these descriptions are of rurality in the United Kingdom, or even more specifically, England and Wales; the UK needs to be put into perspective, particularly in comparison to the rest of Europe:

> *The United Kingdom is one of the most urbanised countries in Europe, and England is the most urbanised part of the Kingdom. Rural England is vulnerable not least because it is so accessible. There is hardly a place in this country that would not fall within the city limits if it were in the United States, hardly a farm more than 30 miles from a major town or city.* (Department of the Environment *et al.*, 1995)

Because there is such a sense of England being an urban environment, it is no surprise that the Rural White Paper (1995) was the first major review by government of rural life. The profile of rural communities does not attract the same degree of attention as urban centres. The Archbishop of Canterbury commissioned a study into urban priority areas that resulted in *Faith in the City*, a report published in 1985 that was widely acclaimed to effectively promote greater Church action in urban areas. It was not until 1990 that a comparable report, *Faith in the Countryside*, was published reflecting on the Church in rural areas.

An urbanised view of the countryside will tend to view rural life as something different yet something to enjoy, if not as participants, then as observers. This view is typified by the Rural White Paper:

> *The countryside is a national asset. The three quarters of us who live in urban areas value it and enjoy it as visitors and weekenders. Those of us who do not live in the countryside must respect the way of life of those who do, the men and women who live and work there. We must understand and respect their different values and priorities.* (Department of the Environment *et al.*, 1995)

Research in rural areas requires an understanding of the complex issues surrounding public and private notions of rurality and how powerful symbolic images of the countryside have informed our understanding of rural life.

Public perceptions of country life have tended to be dominated by idealised images of an unchanging 'picture postcard' rural scene. The reality is that rural areas have undergone vast upheaval and change in the twentieth century. This combination of idealised image and substantial change has been recognised in the Rural White Paper. The opening lines of the document state:

> The enduring character of England is most clearly to be found in the countryside. Yet the pace of change has quickened and much of what we most value about the rural scene seems threatened by increasing mobility, the pressures of leisure and recreation, the decline of jobs in rural industries and the demands for new jobs in businesses which once would have been found only in the towns.
> (Department of the Environment *et al.*, 1995)

The increased mechanisation of agriculture and its decline as the major rural employer, coupled with the rise of tourism and increased environmental concerns, have had a profound effect not just on the physical landscape, but also in socioeconomic terms.

Symptoms of rural drift as people left rural areas for urban ones are now tempered by counter-urbanisation as incomers, particularly the wealthy and retired, increasingly buy into a rural idyll and inhabit rural communities. They bring with them urban lifestyles and financial independence, which allows them freedom of access to services and employment beyond the confines of their rural environment. The resulting colonisation of many rural communities has exacerbated the decline in rural services.

Tourism has also become a powerful shaper of rural areas, bringing much-needed employment. However, its seasonal nature, often coupled with low wages and insecure conditions, can be a disadvantage. Tourism itself thrives and trades on particular images of the countryside and has tended to reinforce romantic, nostalgic views of rurality.

Romantic notions of rural life have profound repercussions for certain groups and individuals living within rural communities. Rural life has been cherished and idealised, and notions of close-knit communities leading happy healthy lives in an idyllic environment have become a powerful representation of rural life:

> Rural areas by their very nature represent places where happy, healthy lifestyles are lived and therefore are symbolised as relatively problem free. (Cloke *et al.*, 1995)

This can have the effect of silencing and obscuring the voices of many rural dwellers, and particularly the rural poor.

DEFINING POVERTY

As with the concept of 'rural', 'poverty' is a contested notion, with protagonists advancing conflicting notions of absolute and relative poverty.

This fact is succinctly illustrated by two quotations in a book reviewing poverty in Britain (Alcock, 1993):

> Poverty means going short materially, socially and emotionally. It means spending less on food, on heating and on clothing than someone on average income ... Above all, poverty takes away the tools to build the blocks for the future – your 'life chances'. It steals away the opportunity to have a life unmarked by sickness, a decent education, a secure home and a long retirement. (Oppenheim, 1990)

> The evidence of improving living standards over this century is dramatic, and it is incontrovertible. When the pressure groups say that one-third of the population is living in poverty, they cannot be saying that one-third of people are living below the draconian subsistence levels used by Booth and Rowntree. (Moore, 1989)

Alcock uses these two quotations to show that poverty as a concept is fundamentally a political viewpoint and is therefore contested. What is being contested is the bench mark by which poverty is measured and assessed. The viewpoint typified by Oppenheim looks for bench marks based around average incomes and/or benefit levels and often the relationship between the two. Critically, what is considered is whether benefit payments or an average income offer an acceptable income, i.e. one that allows someone to experience a standard of living that is considered to be normal within society. Because much of this is often regarded as subjective, such bench marks are difficult to establish. However, once they are, then poverty is assessed as falling below those bench marks.

The view typified by Moore also looks for bench marks by which to assess poverty but they are set against historical or developing world experiences. Thus, the experiences of Victorian England or the standard of living in parts of Africa are perceived as the true face of poverty. Such a viewpoint will tend to deny the concept of poverty in the UK as any experience here can be dismissed through comparison to experiences in the past or elsewhere in the world.

Despite the difficulties in trying to establish an agreed measurement for poverty, there have been numerous attempts to do so. There are strong reasons why a definition and way of measuring poverty is sought; one compelling reason is that once poverty is defined and identified it demands a response:

Poverty is not just a state of affairs, it is an unacceptable state of affairs – it implicitly contains the question, what are we going to do about it? (Alcock, 1993)

Consequently, the desire to identify and measure the true nature and depth of poverty is often inextricably linked to the desire to see something done about it. One of the first and most influential attempts to define and respond was in the work conducted by Booth and Rowntree in Victorian England. Their work focused on the concept of absolute poverty where the ability to avoid starvation, find adequate shelter or maintain basic good health is constrained by a lack of income. Rowntree set the poverty line as lacking the money to 'provide the minimum of food, clothing and shelter needful for the maintenance of merely physical health' (Rowntree, 1902).

A definition of absolute poverty, with its focus on the ability to sustain life, does not itself capture the subtle nuances of social life and the significance of low income as a barrier to full participation and social inclusion. Relative poverty as defined by Townsend (1979) encompasses not just the absolute of basic requirements to sustain life, but also the cultural needs individuals and families require to sustain them within the norms and expectations of their society:

Individuals, families and groups in the population can be said to be in poverty when they lack the resources to obtain the types of diet, participate in the activities and have the living conditions and amenities which are customary, or are at least widely encouraged or approved, in the societies to which they belong.

A lack of resources, principally but not exclusively the lack of financial resources, is the main contributory factor to someone experiencing poverty. In 1994 in the UK there were 9.9 million people living in households receiving Income Support; of these, 3.1 million were children (Department of Social Security, 1995). Using a poverty line of income below 140% of Income Support, Oppenheim (1993) states that in 1989, 3.78 million children in the UK were on the margins of or living in poverty. By 1992/93, this figure had risen to 4.1 million (Oppenheim *et al.*, 1996).

However, even these figures can be contested and subject to changes in benefit payments and entitlement, which in turn are subject to political influences. With such fluctuating and difficult-to-establish definitions and measurements, one response is to focus on deprivation, which is a broader concept than poverty, but with low income and poverty as components of deprivation. Even then, it is important to recognise the significance of a low income:

Poverty is not only about shortage of money. It is about rights and relationships; about how people are treated and how they regard themselves; about powerlessness, exclusion, and loss of dignity. Yet the lack of an adequate income is at its heart. (Archbishop's Commission on Urban Priority Areas, 1985)

If the heart of the issue for the Archbishop's Commission on Urban Priority Areas was income, for the Child Poverty Action Group (CPAG) the heart lies elsewhere:

CPAG is in no doubt about the existence, growth and nature of poverty in the United Kingdom today. At its heart, poverty is about exclusion from social participation. (Oppenheim, 1993)

Even with these differing emphases, it is clear that low income and the ability to participate in the life of community, neighbourhood and society are inextricably linked. Even more so, that the lack of an adequate income can result in exclusion from full citizenship.

Although there may be dispute over what constitutes an adequate income, and over any responses to identified need, for children there is an internationally recognised standard. Article 27 of the United Nations Convention on the Rights of the Child (1991) – to which Britain is a signatory – is very clear that the issue of childhood poverty is not one solely concerned with the maintenance of life, but also embraces the need for children to participate and develop socially within the society in which they live, maintaining:

> ... the right of every child to a standard of living adequate for the child's physical, mental, spiritual, moral and social development.

RURAL POVERTY

If 'rural' and 'poverty' are difficult-to-define and contested terms, then 'rural poverty' is a particularly difficult concept to define and focus attention on. Although poverty is a much debated issue, rural poverty is a less considered problem. For example, the CPAG publication *Poverty: The Facts* (Oppenheim, 1993) covers poverty as a concept and a reality extensively, but covers rural poverty in one page. *Faith in the City* had an entire chapter on poverty, work and employment; in contrast, *Faith in the Countryside* confined itself to a brief section on the distribution of wealth. Most significantly, the Rural White Paper (1995) does not use the word 'poverty' at all and barely gives any attention to deprivation.

Poverty in rural areas tends to be hidden in various ways, not least by the persistence of the popular notion of rural idyll which portrays the countryside not only as an ideal place to live, but as an antidote to urban deprivation. With such an idealised view of the countryside, notions of poverty are unwelcome:

> Historical ideas of the 'rural idyll' have been used discursively as a counterpoint to the problematic nature of many urban areas ... in such circumstances, ideas of poverty in rural areas are anathema both politically and culturally. (Cloke *et al.*, 1995)

Raising the concept of rural poverty is made all the more difficult by the absence of an official poverty line. Without a universally agreed standard that could be applied in rural and urban settings, various indicators of poverty are set according to a range of data. However, rural poverty can also be hidden or obscured statistically. Data (including census data) is not sensitive enough to pick up particular rural situations:

Much of the data available, for example on levels of income and wealth, tends to be aggregated into administrative areas (districts, counties, regions) which can only very crudely be related to areas which can be thought of as rural. (Cloke *et al.*, 1995)

Unlike urban areas where poverty can be clustered in inner cities and peripheral estates, rural poverty is not an area phenomenon but rather consists of marginalised groups of deprived people whose experiences are obscured by the relative affluence of others around them.

Poverty indicators are also heavily biased towards an urban model of deprivation, a good example being transport analysis and car ownership. The possession of a car has been used as one of the indicators of an adequate income (Oppenheim, 1993). Lack of car ownership may not be a significant disadvantage in an urban context with relatively extensive public transport. However, in a rural situation, lack of private transport can be a serious disadvantage where ownership of a car is an essential lifeline – even ownership of one car can be misleading in a situation where low income families may be struggling to maintain mobility and access at great cost. This situation has been recognised in the Rural White Paper:

The National Travel Survey shows that in 1991–1993 over two thirds of journeys in rural areas were by car or van compared to the national average of about half. Public transport alternatives are often limited ... people in rural areas may have no choice but to spend a higher proportion of their incomes on cars than people in the cities. (Department of the Environment *et al.*, 1995)

To begin to assess rural poverty more accurately it is necessary to look at indicators of individual living standards rather than area-based indicators alone. For example, more revealing information about car ownership is not just how many people in an area own a car, but what proportion of income is spent on owning and maintaining a car.

Another means of obscuring rural poverty has been the acceptance within policy arenas of the notion of area-based rural deprivation, a catch all term that has come to mean rural problems associated with housing, employment opportunities, service delivery, mobility etc., and is often seen as a symptom of remoteness and the inaccessibility of services. This overemphasis on area-based concepts of rural deprivation has been highlighted by Brian McLaughlin (1985), one of the most influential rural commentators:

> *By focusing the problem analyses and subsequent policy prescriptions on the issue of rural areas as poor places and on questions of service decline per se, the policy debate on rural deprivation has largely ignored crucial questions about the particular groups and individuals within rural areas who gain or lose as a result of service policies.*

McLaughlin was commissioned by the UK government in the early 1980s to conduct a study of deprivation in rural areas based on an examination of lifestyles and living standards of a sample of the population in five selected areas (McLaughlin, 1985). In addition to discovering that 25% of rural households were living in or on the margins of poverty (based on a threshold of 140% of supplementary benefit levels, now Income Support), McLaughlin (1986) made significant observations about the status of low income families:

> *Whilst the data demonstrated the existence of acute problems of availability of and access to housing, employment, transport and public and private services in rural areas, they also clearly demonstrate that these rural problems are not equally distributed across rural society but tend to be concentrated amongst the less well off. Such findings raise important questions about our current interpretations of rural problems.*

Although McLaughlin's work was requested and commissioned by the Department of the Environment, the report was never published. Even so, the work has been influential in the formation of other research studies and examinations of rural poverty. *Faith in the Countryside* stated, 'we are convinced by the arguments in the report to the Department of the Environment by McLaughlin' (Archbishop's Commission on Rural Areas, 1990).

In 1990, another significant study, *Lifestyles in Rural England* (Cloke *et al.*, 1994b) was initiated, which also sought to draw out the experiences of people living in or on the margins of poverty. As with McLaughlin, the lifestyles study also sought to assess the degree of poverty in rural areas and examined how people's lives were affected by poverty, not least by other people's attempts to ignore its existence:

> Those who do not experience hardship will tend to deny the difficulties of those who do in an attempt to reproduce a learned culture of rural life which filters out the possibilities of poverty and disadvantage in the rural arena.

Paradoxically, people in rural villages can be highly visible and yet their need and hardship can be invisible. Pride, self-reliance and fear of social stigma can all inhibit the articulation of need. In an environment of increasing affluence and plenty, the experience of poverty is compounded by marginalisation and the effects of living physically and socially entwined with more affluent neighbours, resulting in what Newby (1985) has described as two nations in one village.

LISTENING TO CHILDREN AND YOUNG PEOPLE

> The problems experienced by children and young people in the countryside have been an often mentioned but rarely researched component of our understanding of rural lifestyles. (Cloke *et al.*, 1994a)

The guiding principle of this research has been to provide an opportunity for children and young people to reveal their experiences of country life, and to express their needs and desires. The popular concepts of rural childhood are often formed by the reflections of adults looking back on their own rural childhoods imbued with a nostalgic longing for a time of lost innocence. There have been attempts to look at rural childhood less romantically and consider the disadvantages as well as the pleasures of rural life. Colin Ward's book *The Child in the Country* (1988) remains one of the few works that have tried to assess the true nature of rural childhood.

It is probably the youth work agencies that have been most active in trying to raise the profile of rural young people and publications such as *Shadows of Adolescence* (Kennedy, 1984) and the descriptively titled *Nothing Ever Happens Around Here* (Phillips *et al.*, 1994) have gone some way to redressing the balance.

But how children and young people today find life within rural communities, and what pressing issues and concerns they experience, is an area where there is room for much further research. Children are rarely asked for their thoughts and feelings; often adults are presumed to be able to speak for them and opportunities for them to speak for themselves are rarely provided. Even worse, where children's voices are heard, they may well be dismissed if what they say is uncomfortable for adults to hear.

CHILDREN IN RURAL AREAS

In rural areas, children and young people find themselves in a very particular social environment where there may be powerful adult groups whose interests can dominate in a struggle for space and resources; where children and young people can be socially very visible and yet find their needs both invisible and unmet. The effect of this situation has not gone unrecognised:

> *Children in rural areas often lead quite isolated and lonely lives with few opportunities to develop social skills or to widen their interests.* (Duke of Westminster, 1995)

> *The difference for young people in rural areas lies not in the extent of the deprivation but with the reality that the evidence of unrealised potential among young people is already recognised in urban areas whereas it often remains hidden in rural settings.* (Phillips *et al.*, 1994)

For children on a low income, these effects are heightened by their lack of an adequate income and many find themselves pushed to the margins of their communities through social and structural exclusion.

THE SETTING FOR THE RESEARCH

The research was conducted in Somerset and specifically in the West Somerset area. According to the index of rurality established by Cloke, West Somerset is defined as 'extreme rural'. The area also embraces much of the Exmoor National Park and has Areas of Outstanding Natural Beauty within its boundaries. The West Somerset coast is on the Bristol Channel and has suffered from the decline of a major working harbour. Now tourism is the main pull into the area partly due to the Exmoor park and the Quantock hills, but also due to the presence of a large holiday camp. There is also a significant number of caravan sites along the coastline.

The principal towns are Minehead, Watchet and Williton, all of which have populations of less than 10,000. The definition of a rural settlement according to the Rural Development Commission is a settlement with a population of less than 10,000. The nearest urban towns according to that definition are Bridgwater and Taunton.

The Rural Development Commission (RDC) is one of three countryside agencies established by the government; the other two are The Countryside Commission and English Nature. The RDC is the government's statutory adviser on the economic and social development of rural areas in England. The RDC encourages economic regeneration in certain rural areas designated as Rural Development Areas (RDAs). These areas are established where an area is considered to be disadvantaged; the RDC relies heavily upon census data to determine what areas are selected as RDAs. Much of the south west of England is designated as an RDA.

The indicators used by the RDC (1994) to assess whether an area is sufficiently disadvantaged to make it an RDA include:

- persistent high unemployment;

- low male and/or female activity rates, low pay and seasonality of employment;

- a narrow industrial and employment structure resulting in over dependence on a few sources of employment, limited job choice, etc;

- the decline or disappearance of local services and the difficulties of access by those who are less mobile or without access by car to services provided increasingly in larger centres;

- the disadvantage experienced by some individuals or groups within small communities, particularly as a result of their location in rural areas.

Somerset as a county has two Rural Development Areas within it that make up over 50% of the county; West Somerset RDA is where the majority of the research took place.

Somerset County Council has attempted to assess need within the county and in particular rural need. Through research based largely on census data, it carried out a rural needs analysis that revealed West Somerset, and in particular the coastal area of West Somerset, as being in greatest need (Somerset County Council, 1995). One of the indicators used in this analysis was children in low income households, which was an attempt to gain greater awareness of the distribution of low income families in the county of Somerset.

There is generally within the county, both in terms of the County Council and the RDA, an awareness of the need to understand more fully the nature and extent of rural poverty. A follow up to the Somerset Rural Needs Analysis was commissioned by Somerset County Council in 1996. The area also benefited from the presence of the Rt Revd Richard Lewis, who until the end of 1996 was Bishop of Taunton and had been a member of the Archbishop's Commission on Rural Areas.

Somerset, and West Somerset in particular, could fairly represent the concept of the rural idyll, the place to visit, to retire, to escape the urban lifestyle. These areas also represent the growing interest and concern about rural disadvantage and the developing awareness of rural poverty. However, even then there is the risk that the focus is on area concepts of deprivation rather than people's experiences of poverty. Some of the research interviews took place with families in desperate circumstances, with low incomes, little chance of changing their situation and a deep sense of alienation from the rest of the village. Their village fell outside of the RDA, was not highlighted within the rural needs analysis and would be unlikely to present itself as a village with significant need by any census-based research.

Unless people, as well as statistical analysis, become the focus of research our understanding will remain limited. Children and young people will only have an opportunity to express their concerns and aspirations if they are asked.

RESEARCH METHODS

The research was carried out using the following methods.

1. INTERVIEWS WITH CHILDREN AND YOUNG PEOPLE

The aim of the research was not to accumulate statistical data but to draw out children's and young people's own perceptions of rural life.

To facilitate this aim, the questionnaire contained no tick boxes but a series of prompt questions to encourage free response whilst enabling comparative analysis. All children were interviewed in the same way using the same questionnaire regardless of income status – low income children were not treated differently in the process.

Children's and young people's voices were central to the research process and the aim was to ensure that children and young people had the opportunity to speak for themselves, and that their accounts of their lives were acknowledged, supported and respected. An important aim of the research was to provide an opportunity for children on a low income to talk about their experiences and to gain some insight and understanding of their lives.

95 children were interviewed of whom 42 were known to be on a low income.

For the purposes of this research, low income was defined as those children whose families were in receipt of Income Support and were receiving free school meals. The use of free school meals as an indicator is in itself problematic, a situation recognised by the Child Poverty Action Group:

> Some families with children do not take up their entitlement to income support and some families with children who are receiving income support do not take up their entitlement to free school meals. (Oppenheim, 1993)

Anecdotal information from some families suggested that in certain situations the stigma attached to receiving a free school meal when most children in the school did not was enough to discourage take up. In addition, entitlement to free school meals does not take into account low wages or seasonal work so that some families may be entitled to free school meals during part of the year but not the whole.

Consequently, it is likely that the figure of 42 children on a low income is an under representation of the total number of children interviewed who were from a low income household. However, the free school meal indicator did give an assurance that those children were on a low income and it should be seen as a baseline indicator of poverty.

The age range was from 8 to 19 years, but with the majority in the 11 to 15 age range; interviews were conducted in a variety of settings in West Somerset.

These settings varied from a family home to a youth club but the majority of interviews were carried out in schools. All interviews contributed to the analysis of what children were saying about rural life and the impact of low incomes. However, to ensure complete accuracy in the verbatim quotes, only those taped interviews that were clear enough to allow verbatim reproduction are used. Consequently, the majority of quotes are from the school-based interviews; the youth club and family home environments proved to be less conducive to taping interviews.

Interviews were conducted using a semi-structured format covering opportunities for play and association, school activities, friendships, transport and accessibility. Children were also asked for their perceptions of rural and town life, and how they experienced life in their own communities, including their perceptions of power and the capacity for change.

In accordance with the aims of the research, interviews were conducted in an informal manner and although prompt questions were used to enable comparative analysis of data, respondents were encouraged to talk freely and openly about their own experiences, issues and concerns. As the research is composed of qualitative rather than quantitative data, the emphasis is on what children say. Where figures and statistics are used, they reflect those responses that are clear and obvious. No figures are used on the basis of what children imply in their responses.

Most of the interviews were carried out in three schools – a small village primary school, a middle school drawing from a rural area, and a large secondary community school with a wide rural catchment area. The advantage of interviewing in school was that a wide range of communities were covered. Some children were from small hamlets, others from villages and others from the principal rural centres in the area.

Children and young people were interviewed mainly in pairs and where possible low income children were paired together. The majority of interviews were tape recorded, although some interviews in the youth club were conducted using a note taker.

Steps were taken to ensure that the children and young people were in a position to make an informed choice about participation and about the use of a tape recorder.

All of the children's names have been changed to protect their anonymity, and each verbatim quote contains a 'name' and the age of the child respondent. In addition, the names of small towns and villages mentioned by some of the children have been left out of their quotes where there was any possibility of the child being identified through them.

2. INTERVIEWS WITH PROFESSIONALS

During the early stages of the research, interviews were conducted with a range of 35 professionals in West Somerset (including councillors and council officials, youth workers, community education officers, social services, health visitors, voluntary agencies and church representatives). These interviews were conducted on a face-to-face basis and were a valuable aid to ascertaining the views and perceptions of professionals working with children and young people in rural areas, and the perspectives of other service providers working in rural communities.

One aspect became clear as a result of these interviews: it is difficult for many agencies to have an accurate knowledge of poverty and how it impacts upon children. More often, the overriding concern is about the impact of rurality and the notion of rural deprivation. The issue of poverty as a specific issue rarely features as a primary focus of either statutory or voluntary groups. This is not due to a lack of concern or interest – both were apparent in the agency interviews – but the absence of informed analysis of the nature and extent of poverty within the area as a whole.

3. INTERVIEWS WITH FAMILIES

Interviews were also carried out with eight families living on a low income in West Somerset. These interviews were carried out informally in people's homes, and gave a valuable insight into the experiences and preoccupations of parents bringing up children on a low income in the countryside. Their experiences of struggling to maintain their families on a low income would be worthy of further research in itself. They highlighted the difficulties of trying to own and run a car or cope with the inadequacies of public transport. For example, one parent described the arrangement she had made with a local garage to pay off repair bills in instalments. Another described the frustration of not being able to send her child to school for the first few weeks of school life because reception classes took children for mornings only initially and the school bus did not do a midday return journey.

The attention given to rural families often centres around issues of childcare. Various childcare initiatives have been set up in recent years and with rural disadvantage in mind. The RDC commissioned a rural childcare initiative that sought to demonstrate the need for better rural childcare and support demonstration projects that promote good practice. This work was written up and a guide to good rural childcare was published in 1996 (Rural Development Commission). This guide focused on 15 schemes throughout England and presented them as examples of good rural childcare provision.

However, out of the 15 projects, not one stated that it offered any concessions to low income families. Two of the schemes were mobile and one of these stated that there were no charges made to parents in order to ensure no one was excluded. Another scheme incorporated a local authority day nursery and another had concessions for four-year-olds who attended a playgroup. But overall, the concession made towards low income families is minimal. The limitation of many rural childcare schemes is that they relate primarily to parents who are working or involved in training; they offer very little to parents who are on benefits. The government supports childcare initiatives that focus on employment or training opportunities for parents (Department of the Environment *et al.*, 1995). While this is laudable, it is not addressing the needs of low income families.

Structure of the report

Throughout the report, each chapter will look at the wider issues raised during our interviews and will then draw out the experiences of children and young people who are on a low income.

In chapter 2, children and young people reflect on their lives in the countryside, and what images and perceptions they have of country and town life. They also indicate whether they would rather live in the country or the town. From their accounts, it is apparent that for some children and young people there are great benefits to be derived from a country lifestyle. However, it was also clear that children's experiences of rural life vary, and that other factors such as age and income status affect how children and young people feel about living in rural areas.

Chapter 3 looks at opportunities for play and association. Children talk about the opportunities they feel are available to them, what clubs or activities they are able to participate in and what difficulties, if any, they experience in attending. From their responses, it is apparent that there is a considerable lack of structured provision, and what is available often lacks variety and appeal for young people. Difficulties with access and mobility are emerging themes. Again, age is a factor and for children and young people on a low income, scarcity of provision and difficulties in access were compounded by financial constraints.

Chapter 4 looks at the provision of after-school activities and classes. There was a dearth of opportunities and difficulties in access due to transportation and the effects of widespread rural catchment areas. For low income respondents, cost was an important factor operating to exclude them from participation and, where there was no statutory provision of concessionary places to facilitate involvement, they experienced structural exclusion from the few opportunities available.

Chapter 5 looks at children and young people's ability to make and sustain friendships in a rural environment where opportunities to meet and associate with peers can be considerably reduced. Transport difficulties were again instrumental in reducing contact and had a particular impact on maintaining school friendships out of school. However, access to transport was a considerable advantage and this section highlights the different resources available to children, with low income children having least resources and greatest difficulty in sustaining friendships.

Chapter 6 explores the issue of transport and mobility. Difficulties associated with transport and mobility is one of the factors most frequently associated with rural disadvantage, and access to private transport ensures that dependence on dwindling and inadequate public transport is minimal. Children in general suffer limited mobility and a high dependence on adults, and this can create conflict. However, transportation was not a burning issue where children and young people had access to one or two cars. What was starkly apparent from the responses was the disparity between low income children's access to private transport and that of their more affluent peers. Low income children and young people revealed a high dependence on public transport and therefore suffered disproportionately from problems of scarcity and costly and inadequate provision.

Chapter 7 looks at unsupervised play opportunities and social space. It examines issues of visibility within communities and how children can be seen as problems, and the conflict which may arise with adults and the elderly over resources and social space. Children reported feelings of powerlessness and the sense that their needs are secondary to those of adults. Again, age was a factor as teenagers felt less welcome in their communities. These problems were compounded for children and young people on a low income who, in many cases, lacked the resources to fulfil their social needs beyond their immediate environment and were therefore contained and highly visible within their communities.

The conclusion draws together the main findings of the research and highlights the important themes that have emerged from children's responses. What is apparent is that whilst all rural children potentially suffer from problems associated with poor service provision, isolation and restricted mobility, those with access to sufficient income, transport, land etc. are able to overcome these disadvantages and enjoy a satisfactory rural lifestyle. In contrast, those children and young people in rural areas on a low income experience a qualitatively different type of rural childhood. Poverty in the countryside is a marginalising experience, often both hidden and denied. What is clearly apparent in children's responses is the dual impact of rurality and low income, resulting in many cases in physical and social isolation and exclusion.

THE VOICES OF CHILDREN AND YOUNG PEOPLE

Although interviews with adults and professionals gave an important insight into service delivery in rural areas and provided an adult perspective on rural children's lives, the primary aim of the research was always to provide a medium through which children and young people could speak for themselves about their lives and experiences. Therefore, all quotations used are taken verbatim from children's and young people's responses. They provide a richly descriptive picture of rural childhood and a rare insight into the particular experiences of children on a low income.

CHAPTER *2*

Country life

Public perceptions of rural childhood have been informed largely by adults and in particular by the reflective, idealised accounts of writers looking back at their own rural childhoods through a somewhat rose-tinted lens.

Listening to how rural children themselves view their lives is more likely to bring meaning to our understanding of rural life.

LIVING IN THE COUNTRYSIDE

In this chapter children speak for themselves about what it means for them to live in the countryside and what images and perceptions they have about life in a town. Children and young people were asked a series of questions about whether they felt they lived in the countryside and what life in the countryside meant to them. They were also asked about their perceptions of town life, if they felt life was different in a town, whether they would rather live in a town than in the countryside and why.

Do you feel like you live in the countryside ?

Of those 85 who responded, the majority – 72% (61) felt that they did, while 28% (24) felt that they did not. The reasons why not varied but the sense of a lack of remoteness was a common theme.

Would you rather live in a town ?

Of those 78 who responded, 63% (49) said 'no' and 37% (29) said 'yes'. What constituted a town for these children varied, but most children regarded places like Taunton and Bridgwater as representing the nearest town. Some children in the remotest areas saw smaller but nearer settlements as towns.

IMPRESSIONS OF COUNTRY AND TOWN LIFE

Seventy children and young people responded to both the above questions. Their attitudes and perceptions of town and country living tended to fall into subgroups, with the two main groups – those who felt they lived in the country and did not want to live in the town, and those who felt they lived in the country and would rather live in the town – showing very different attitudes towards their lives.

RURAL BLISS

When looked at in combination, 51% (37) children tended to think they lived in the countryside and liked it; this was the 'rural bliss' group. They did not want to live in the town and had a very positive attitude towards the countryside.

For many of these children, popular concepts of country dwelling and the rural idyll were most likely to be reflected in their accounts, and their experiences of country life are comfortably enmeshed with their understanding of what rural life embodies.

The lifestyle descriptions used by these children contained powerful symbolic images similar to those that inform public discourse around the notion of rural life. Descriptions gave an overall picture of peace and quiet, images of fields, trees, fresh air, space and beauty. Opportunities for seeing wildlife and the presence of farm animals were appreciated and enjoyed. There was also a significant emphasis expressed by some of these children on the benefits of having less traffic and consequently less fumes and pollution. This observation was most often expressed in direct contrast to town or city life, which was viewed very negatively.

For many of these children, the positive benefits of rural life were clearly in evidence showing that for some children the rural idyll is closer to a reality than a myth:

You can take nice long walks ... make rope swings in the woods.
(Jane, aged 13)

Not many cars, it doesn't smell like in the big towns, you can play around in the fields and stuff and there's lots of animals.
(James, aged 11)

[Home village] *is like a memory place for me. I know all the places to go and stuff, and most of 'ems in the woods.* (Tom, aged 13)

When I was five, I moved up here from the city and I find it more peaceful in the countryside 'cos there's not too much pollution and noise. (Sarah, aged 13)

Not all fumes going outside your door all the time. (Tanya, aged 11)

On a bike you can go somewhere without getting knocked over. (David, aged 13)

These accounts taken alone would strongly support the image of the countryside as an environment ideally suited for children. For some, the opportunity to live in the countryside has many benefits and children themselves are able to appreciate these. However, this is not the complete picture and it can obscure the experiences of other children.

For children with a rural bliss approach, images of town life were mainly negative and in response to whether town life was different to rural life they were clear that it was not only different, but also much less desirable.

Noise and pollution were frequently mentioned and the over-whelming impression was of too many people, houses and cars creating a lack of space and freedom. There was also an impression of danger being present in towns although, as shall be shown later, this was mainly confined to those children on a low income:

Lots of people, lots of cars and lots of shops all squashed in one place, there's too much of it ... All the stuff put into one thing and no room for everybody. (Jim, aged 13)

Well, there wouldn't be any trees and probably my lifestyle would be totally different – I wouldn't be able to run anywhere and there wouldn't be any fields to play in. (Lisa, aged 13)

There's nothing there, there's no countryside really, no fields or anything – it's just buildings. (Scott, aged 13)

Because I like it here I wouldn't want to be in a place that has so much traffic. (Susan, aged 12)

It's more peaceful and less dangerous in the countryside than it is in the town. (David, aged 13)

However, these experiences of rural life and the accompanying perceptions of urban life are not universal to all children – others have quite different views.

URBAN BLISS

The second most numerous group (17 children) consisted of those who felt they did live in the countryside but were less happy with it and would rather live in the town. This was the 'urban bliss' group. From these children and young people a very different perception of country living emerged.

There were similarities with the former group about what living in the countryside meant, and references to animals, wildlife, lack of pollution and peace and quiet were mentioned. However, overlaying this was a sense of boredom and the feeling that there was nothing to do. Quietness and the presence of fewer people were regarded as negative attributes rather than positive ones.

Some children also showed an awareness of other people's perceptions of country childhood:

[They] *think there are loads of places to explore, but when you've lived here a long time you've explored them all.* (Tasha, aged 15)

You've just got like loads of hills and stuff where people come and see. There's not really much for young people to do – it's all for like the older generation. (Laura, aged 15)

Difficulties with travel and accessibility were emerging themes. One girl talks about the community she lives in as being quiet and peaceful but also out of balance, with a preponderance of elderly people. For her, access to activities meant organising everything a week ahead and travel to events was fraught with problems:

The thing is there aren't any buses. There's like one every hour and they don't fit in with the cinema times, and you find that you either get there really early and you can't get a bus back, or it's the other way round. (Katie, aged 13)

For these children and young people, the town's potential to relieve their boredom and allow them freedom of access meant that they expressed none of the cautious or disparaging views displayed by the first group.

Pollution, noise levels and overcrowding were not important considerations. Town life was good and full of opportunities to meet with friends, go out with greater ease and have access to shops and activities:

> There's more things to do, more places to go and more people to be with. (Gemma, aged 13)

> If you did live in [local town] it'd be only £2 to go down to [an amusement park]. You could walk there and walk back and not have to pay for bus fares. (Sally, aged 13)

Several respondents felt that they would rather live on the outskirts of a large town and thereby keep some of the benefits of country life whilst enjoying the greater freedom of access afforded by the town:

> It would be easier, I'd wanna live on the outskirts of town ... get the best of both worlds. (Victoria, aged 15)

For a few children, the issue of privacy emerged. These children contrasted the lack of privacy and heightened visibility they were experiencing in their rural communities with the perceived anonymity of town life. Sally explains the advantages for her of living in the town:

> You can even do something without the rest of the town knows. (Sally, aged 13)

Easier access to housing and employment was also a factor:

> You can get to work easier and you don't have to travel – my mum's often late home from work, usually she has to do overtime. (Peter, aged 13)

THOSE WHO DID NOT FEEL THAT THEY LIVED IN THE COUNTRYSIDE

Of the 85 who responded to the question 'Do you feel like you live in the countryside?', 24 felt that they did not. This group also tended to fall into two subgroups consisting of those who would or would not prefer to live in a town, although responses here were less clear cut.

Respondents came from a wide variety of areas and their reasons for feeling they did not live in the countryside were often due to the physical proximity of roads and housing, which was in direct contrast to their perceptions of what living in the countryside means. These perceptions often consisted of romantic images of rural lifestyles which did not fit with their own experiences. Mark explains why he does not feel as if he lives in the country:

Not really ... 'cos there's loads of housing and it doesn't feel like the country.

Living in the countryside for him would mean:

It's quite lovely ... [you] could go for really long walks.
(Mark, aged 11)

Another boy of thirteen explains that he has no fields to play in whereas living in the countryside would mean:

One house on top of a hill with no one else. (Steve, aged 13)

The views and the way it's laid out, it's beautiful. (Donna, aged 12)

There are also signs of a conflict of interests between young people and tourism, which in this instance affects their experiences of rural life:

The queues on the road are really long. [Whereas] *if someone said to me like would you like to live in the country, I'd sort of think of a couple of houses in the middle of nowhere, and long windy roads and stuff.* (Becky, aged 12)

We've got holiday-makers down around where we live and it's like a bit noisy and it's not like living in the countryside ... Come down into the town and it's really hard to move around, there's loads of people. (Carla, aged 12)

Those who wished to live in the town expressed similar reasons as the 'urban bliss' group, citing more activities and more people. However, this group did not feel that they lived in the countryside either. They were altogether more ambivalent about their situation but urban areas had more appeal with accessibility an important plus for town life:

> They've got like loads of shops and stuff and then they can go up there after school and stuff, but we can't like buy anything 'cos our dad's at work and we've got no transport to get there.

(Mark, aged 11)

Of those who did not wish to live in a town, several wanted to live somewhere more akin to their images of the countryside.

AGE AS A FACTOR

The age of respondents was a significant factor when asked if they would rather live in a town.

78 children responded to this question.

49 said they would not want to live in a town; of these, 84% were below 14 years of age and 16% were 14 years and above.

29 said they would rather live in a town; of these, 52% were below 14 years of age and 48% were 14 years and above.

The proportion of children wanting to live in a town increases as they get older. These findings may well reflect the very particular demands of youth culture. Opportunities for peer group association, to see and be seen, are critical; the ability to follow the fashions and fads of the time are seen as vital in maintaining credibility and allowing self-expression.

For many rural young people, access to events and peer group gatherings is often severely restricted and difficulties with transport can impact on many areas of their lives. These young people talk about the desire to get out, meet more people, and the need for clubs and excitement.

This attitude in many instances coincides with attendance at senior schools where children are drawn from large, spatially-spread catchment areas. For many rural young people, this is their first contact with town dwellers and they may develop an acute awareness of what other young people are doing after school. Friendships made in this environment often prove difficult to maintain outside of school time. This issue is picked up later in chapter 7.

Rural life on a low income

Children on a low income in rural areas would appear to share similar experiences of rurality with other children. However, poverty is a relative experience which can influence the way in which children view their environment. The effects are felt both in the immediacy of daily life and over time. Low income children's responses to questions about what country life means to them and their perceptions of town life revealed qualitatively different lifestyle experiences from their more affluent counterparts.

Of those children not wishing to live in the town, low income children – particularly the younger ones – were most likely to mention fears and dangers associated with town living. This conceivably reflects a lack of security in life generally, manifested in a fear of the unknown. The reality may well be that life is inherently more threatening and insecure for those children, who do not have the financial security to cushion themselves from the harsher aspects of life.

The following accounts are all from children and young people on a low income:

I wouldn't want to live in a town 'cos there's loads of cars 'n that and you hear about all the rough things that go on in the towns 'n that. (Cheryl, aged 13)

That's where most of the robbers go. (Susan, aged 11)

People here are mostly friendly but in [local town] *they can be horrible, they can pick on you, they'll do whatever they can just to get something.* (Emma, aged 11)

[You are] *afraid to go out at night.* (Stacey, aged 12)

You never know what they [people in town] *will do to you.* (Rachel, aged 12)

For some of these younger children, the countryside represents a security and a freedom that they did not feel they would have in a town.

More space to live in and more things to do ... 'cos if you step out into the road, ten to one you get killed in the town. (Sarah, aged 13)

> *It's more peaceful and less dangerous in the countryside than it is in the town.* (David, aged 13)

However, for many of the low income respondents, life in the countryside was described in very different terms from those used by the other respondents. These children and young people's descriptions of their lives were imbued with a strong sense of boredom and isolation, with many feeling trapped and constrained by their surroundings:

> *It's just so boring and quiet and nothing to do ... You've just got like loads of hills and stuff where people come and see. There's not really much for young people to do, it's all for like the older generation.* (Laura, aged 15)

> *All shut in and not much to do ... I've got used to it now and it's boring ... It's not so adventurous once you know where everything is.* (Tara, aged 12)

> *I feel like I'm closed in, like kept here ... There ain't nothing to do, it's boring.* (John, aged 13)

> *Sometimes you feel really isolated from the rest of the country.* (Zoe, aged 12)

> *Holidays everyone goes away, they go on holiday.* (Mary, aged 13)

> *It's really boring in the winter 'cos it's dark and horrible an' there's nothing to do and there's not really any jobs for young people.* (June, aged 15)

CONCLUSION

For many, there are undoubted benefits to living in the countryside. Many children express themselves as happy with country life and this is particularly true of younger children. However, for other children, a less comfortable image of country living begins to emerge. There are signs that age is an important mediating factor and indications that there is an age at which life in the countryside can become particularly restrictive.

Visibility and conflict with tourism, and an increasingly elderly rural population, have had an impact on how some children experience and understand rural life. Difficulties with transport and limited access to activities and shops are all emerging themes, and are symptomatic of what we understand to mean by rural deprivation. However, whereas rural deprivation has come to embody the price that people pay for a rural lifestyle, the reality is that these rural problems impact upon certain groups to a much greater degree than upon others.

For children on a low income, the apparent benefits of the countryside are less certain and what is revealed is a qualitatively different experience of rural life as we begin to see the interlocking effects of rurality and low income upon children's lives.

CHAPTER *3*

Opportunities for play and association

For most children, opportunities for play and association with peer groups are essential requirements for personal growth and development. Children's abilities to make and sustain friendships, develop interpersonal skills and explore social relationships are all enhanced by provision of space and opportunity for meeting and associating with other young people.

Often highly visible within their own small communities, rural children and their needs tend to be socially invisible when provisions for play and activities are discussed. In this respect, public notions of rural childhood as an almost ideal state may be influential and effectively work against an understanding of children's needs within the very particular environment that country living creates.

CLUBS

In this part of the research, children discussed the clubs and activities that they felt were available to them within their towns and villages. What was apparent was the general dearth of provision, with many villages providing no social space or structured activities at all. Villages nowadays are rarely able to function as self-sufficient social or economic units and within a village community there is often a considerable struggle to meet the needs of both adults and children. However, as is often the case when resources are scarce, those with the least power will often be the ones to lose out. Children are structurally disadvantaged by their exclusion from power and decision making, and where there is a conflict with adult interests in the use of space and limited facilities, adult interests frequently prevail.

This effect can most often be seen in the provision of a youth club. Whilst many towns and villages do provide a youth club, the reality is that for many children and young people this is often just available for a couple of hours once a week, sometimes under very cramped and restricted circumstances. This environment lends very little to children and young people's need for social space and the ownership of that space. There are often difficulties in securing access to village halls, and there are signs of institutional exclusion by parish councils and village hall committees. Children showed a keen awareness that there is not much available for them:

> I'd like to have more things to do in [home village] 'cos when you get home from school it's either telly or homework. There's not very many things to do after school. (Scott, aged 13)

> There's not a lot really, I mean not in the evenings, I mean I like to go out but there's not a lot you can do. (Katie, aged 13)

However, despite the inadequacy of provision available, for those children where there are no opportunities at all, any provision would be a welcome relief. Children's needs tend to be very basic at this level and they often express a need just for somewhere to meet – their own space. For these children and young people, problems of visibility are exacerbated by a lack of privacy and space in which to meet away from the adult gaze. As Paula explains:

> Well, there's not really anything around [home village]. If there was more, I think people wouldn't be so bored and we wouldn't have to annoy the neighbours so much. (Paula, aged 13)

In larger rural settlements and towns, provision tends to be greater but lacking in variety. What there is is more often orientated towards younger children, with uniformed organisations and sporting clubs being a significant presence. However, not all children are sporting and as some of the girls pointed out, many sporting clubs tend to provide sports typically associated with boys.

OLDER CHILDREN

Older children are particularly badly served and can feel bored and frustrated:

> There wouldn't be anything to do even if we were allowed to.
> (Mary, aged 13)

Like my friend came up this morning and said, 'Are you coming out?' and I said, 'Yeah, all right,' 'cos like usually I just come down here but when we go out we all sort of get together and get dressed up and there's still nothing to do – all we do is just stumble around. (Laura, aged 15)

There are signs that towns and villages are reluctant to provide opportunities for older children to come together and older children are often seen as threatening when gathered together in groups. In one town surveyed where a regular meeting place for young people had been provided, there developed a conflict between the needs of those young people and the interests of the town in attracting tourists. Young people congregating in and around an area where tourists gather became unacceptable and the resulting conflict with authorities meant that they had to look for new premises. Many young people report having to resort to going into pubs and, where available, arcades and holiday camps, often drinking under age.

Sally explains how it works at one holiday camp:

You go in to buy a drink and they say, 'Are you under age?' and you say, 'No, I'm down here on holiday and I'm not under age'. (Sally, aged 13)

Cathy is 14 years old and lives in a small rural town. She reveals her frustration at having nothing to do:

If there's nothing to do, you end up going and getting drunk or something like that ... But then they say, 'Why don't you just be normal?' – but what is there to do, there's nothing to do, is there? (Cathy, aged 14)

TRANSPORT TO CLUBS

Whilst there is an obvious lack of provision and opportunities to access play and social activities, this does not have the same impact upon all groups of children. Those sufficiently affluent and/or sufficiently mobile are able to access a much greater variety of clubs and activities. The ability to reach out beyond their towns and villages and service their social and recreational needs elsewhere means that these children are able to experience the benefits of country living without suffering from many of the disadvantages.

Transport to and from activities can cause considerable difficulty, especially for children living in relatively isolated villages who may not possess their own transport or whose transport is tied up with a parent working away from home. Parents are understandably reluctant to let their children walk to and from clubs along badly-lit roads, and public transport provision is rarely either available or adequate for fitting in with club times:

> *Most of the time I'm walking there and back in the dark and dad doesn't really like that much but it's the only thing I can do.*
> (Jane, aged 13)

Millie explains why she doesn't go to any clubs:

> *It's quite a way to go, it's sort of nine miles and it takes about twenty minutes in the car but in the bus it goes all around the back lanes and it takes about three quarters of an hour.*
> (Millie, aged 14)

THE EFFECTS OF LOW INCOME

Whilst children who were not on a low income were obviously experiencing difficulties with regard to scarcity and quality of provision, it was very rare for them to mention the cost of activities or clubs. When low income children were interviewed, a very different picture emerged and it was apparent that the cost of clubs was an ever-present factor in their perceptions of what was available and in their ability to participate.

Low income children were the least likely to go to a variety of clubs and activities, and youth club was the most frequently mentioned activity. However, even at youth clubs the cost was instrumental in whether some children attended or not.

The following quotations are all from children and young people on a low income:

> *Well, there's a youth club but it's just under a quid to go in a night and they do it two nights a week and I think that's just a bit too expensive.* (Robert, aged 14)

If you just hang around then it's OK and it doesn't cost a lot but it's like if you want to do something like go to youth club, the youth club's 50p and it's not that good a youth club either so it's not worth 50p ... If there were things around here I'm sure they'd cost a lot of money so there isn't really a choice. (Ella, aged 13)

Stacey explains that her youth club has two nights a week but that the prices differ – Tuesdays, 30 pence; Fridays, 50 pence:

I go on Tuesdays, I can only afford to go on Tuesdays.
(Stacey, aged 12)

Where other clubs and activities are available, many low income children did not even consider them an option, especially with clubs that involved the possession of uniforms or the need for equipment:

It [tennis] *costs – you have to hire out a court and 'cos I haven't got my own tennis racquet, I have to hire out a tennis racquet.*
(Lisa, aged 13)

I used to go swimming but it's gone up to nearly two pounds now. (Robert, aged 14)

I'm thinking of going to judo but it's quite dear for all the suits.
(Tom, aged 13)

For many low income children, the chance to meet other children and participate in shared activities can be particularly important, especially when many are unable to afford holidays and other opportunities to move beyond their towns and villages:

There's not a lot of things to do around here ... We don't go on holiday because mum can't afford it. (Carla, aged 12)

CONCLUSION

Although there will be difference and diversity in the way rurality is experienced, what emerges from this research is the significant impact of rural factors upon children and young people. Transport difficulties and scarcity of opportunity and resources, whilst often acknowledged as factors in rural deprivation as it affects adults, are little understood and rarely acknowledged in relation to children. These factors can have a very particular effect upon children's social and cultural needs, exacerbated by children's exclusion from influence and decision making.

Whilst children not on a low income have sufficient affluence and mobility to reach out beyond the confines of their immediate environment and access a variety of activities and opportunities, what emerges in many children's perceptions of their situation is a general poverty of opportunity for play and association and a lack of social space. Provision of clubs and activities in rural areas is characterised by a lack of variety and a continuing struggle to maintain what does exist, coupled with constraints on facilities and difficulties with accessibility. However, whilst these factors can have an impact upon many rural children, children on a low income suffer the additional constraint of financial hardship.

Where there is some provision of clubs or activities, low income children find the cost of participating invariably constrains and reduces involvement. Entrance fees, uniform costs and the availability and cost of transport are all factors that militate against participation. For children in this research, the financial barriers to participating in clubs were often measured in pence rather than pounds. As little as a 50 pence entrance fee was enough to prevent one child from going to a youth club.

Children on a low income who live in areas where there is no provision are also the least likely to be able to access activities beyond their immediate environment. To gain access to services and facilities not within walking distance requires either personal transport or the use of public transport. The issue with public transport is not only its limited availability, but for children on a low income the cost is also an important consideration. As for personal transport, low income children are aware of the restraints on those parents who do have a car in terms of petrol costs and the availability of the car to transport children to and from events.

Other transport options are available in rural areas, such as shared transport and giving lifts. However, in interviews with low income families, the issue of reciprocity was raised. For some parents, their inability to give lifts to other parents' children was sufficiently embarrassing to prevent them from taking up the option themselves.

Frequently in rural areas there has been some recognition of children's need for shared play and peer group activities. However, where the solution has been to provide a facility there has been little understanding or acknowledgement that low income children may well be socially excluded by virtue of the cost. These costs may appear to be minimal but for children on a low income sometimes any cost is enough to prevent them gaining access to a facility that may be the only one within their community.

CHAPTER 4

School activities

For children in rural areas, time at school can be a particularly productive experience, with opportunities to meet and associate with other children and encounter a diversity of experiences and lifestyles. For many children, the step up from junior to senior school may mean travelling for the first time beyond their small towns and villages and into a very different environment.

Rural areas are often characterised by small, spatially-spread communities and secondary schooling tends to embrace a wide catchment area often incorporating both small, isolated hamlets and larger villages and small towns. For many children and young people, this may mean long journeys by bus to attend school coupled with a return to a more isolated environment at the end of the school day. This can have implications both for children's abilities to make and sustain friendships, and for their participation in activities run by the schools. As the research has revealed, opportunities for structural play and peer group association are often severely restricted in rural areas and schools are particularly well-equipped to provide space and opportunities for shared activities.

AFTER-SCHOOL ACTIVITIES

In this part of the research, children and young people talked about their schools as providers of after-school and holiday activities. Children came from a variety of schools, ranging from a small village junior school to a large community secondary school servicing a wide catchment area.

What is apparent from their responses is that some children are able to attend a wide variety of activities and clubs after school but that many children – particularly those on a low income – find difficulty in attending due to problems with transport. For many children, there is also an issue around returning to a school environment in leisure time. Schools can be associated with a particular type of experience involving authority and discipline that does not sit comfortably with notions of free time and leisure activity. Transport to and from activities at school was problematic for some children. Although many activities start just after the school day has finished, children still need transport to get them back to their families when the school bus has gone:

> [I] *know about them but I can't get to them. Most of my friends don't want to do the same things so we can't share lifts.*
> (Scott, aged 13)

> *My mum can't usually bring me 'cos she's usually doing something.* (Jenny, aged 12)

Where activities were available and children were able to access them, they prove a valuable resource, often providing children with a more stimulating and imaginative selection of activities from which to choose. However, cost was an important issue and, as will be apparent when we look at the opportunities for children on a low income to participate, after-school activities are often costly and there is little concession given to enable participation. Where cost and transport difficulties were not an issue, children reported attending a wide variety of activities, both after school and during holiday time. For example, one child attends youth club, Air Training Corps, badminton and football. In the holidays he goes away with the school on trips and also does canoeing, skiing and sailing.

LOW INCOME CHILDREN AND ACCESS TO AFTER-SCHOOL ACTIVITIES

Although some schools operate a reduction system for large families, there is rarely any concessionary payments system in operation for children of families in receipt of Income Support or Family Credit. For children and young people on a low income, the initial cost of participating is often problematic. Responses from low income children showed a high degree of concern about cost. For many of them, there was an ever-present awareness of fees, uniform costs and transport difficulties.

The following accounts are all from children and young people on a low income:

> *I used to do judo and I used to do gym club but after a while I just couldn't ... Each week it costs £1, it soon adds up and then my sister wanted to join as well ... Judo costs about £3 a term but you have to buy all the uniform and that's as well so it's quite expensive.* (Lisa, aged 13)

> *They used to open the swimming pool in the summer but it costs money every hour.* (Tom, aged 13)

> *If my mum lets me go she'd have to let my sister go and my brother ... she'd have to pay for all of us to go.* (Cathy, aged 14)

Linda explains that she would like to go to things at the school but she has great difficulties with transport. Her family live in a small village and her mother cannot afford the petrol to use their car for leisure activities. She is very aware that her friends at school stay on and go to clubs. There are no clubs in her village and she finds the summer months particularly boring:

> *I didn't notice it as much when I was younger.* (Linda, aged 15)

Transport problems can be particularly difficult for young people attending secondary schools to resolve. The distance from school to home may be considerable and some children are expected to pay bus fares and sometimes club fees out of their pocket money:

> *I don't think my mum would really appreciate me staying on after school and coming to pick me up, so all my pocket money would have to go on bus fares back.* (Laura, aged 15)

Paula is very aware of the cost of petrol for her family if she stayed on after school. She explains why she doesn't attend any courses at the school:

> *Some of them are quite expensive and to pick up from here* [school] *and go back to* [home village] *is quite expensive.* (Paula, aged 13)

Low income respondents were particularly aware of transport difficulties and the limitations of relying on the school bus:

> I used to go to some but now there's not so many good things
> going on and as I catch the bus they sometimes go on really late
> and it means walking over the hill and mum doesn't really like me
> walking over the hill. (Carla, aged 12)

CONCLUSION

Due to the shortage of facilities and opportunities available to children
and young people in their home surroundings, schools would seem to
offer a relatively well-equipped and suitable venue for the provision of
clubs and leisure activities.

Where they are able to attend, children show an interest in participating in after-school activities and in doing so they are able to experience a greater variety of choice than they would have open to them
within their own communities. However, after-school activities do not
suit all children. Whilst some are not interested in returning to school
in their free time, others may experience difficulties in accessibility
due to problems with transport. This is particularly likely where children are drawn from a wide catchment area. Classes and clubs can
also be expensive, both for the school to run and also for the families
who have to pay. This can be particularly difficult for larger families
and some schools operate a scheme whereby larger families are eligi-
ble for a reduction in fees.

Where transport to clubs and after-school activities has posed a
problem for some children who are not on a low income, the difficulties
have tended to involve access and availability of transport. For low
income respondents, these problems are overlaid with an awareness of
cost either in petrol or bus fares. There is a strong public perception that
difficulties of access in rural areas can often be resolved by transport
sharing. Some families may well use lift sharing as a means of splitting
the financial and time costs of getting children to and from activities.
However, as will be shown in chapter 6, many families on a low income
do not own a car. As stated in the previous chapter, this creates problems
with reciprocity and many families find themselves unable to enter into
sharing arrangements when they have nothing to share.

Whilst after-school activities appear to offer a greater range and diversity of choice, where there is no concessionary system to assist low income families, children will not be able to avail themselves of this choice. Concessions that offer reduced or free places to children on a low income would go a long way to increasing choice for these children. What is clear from low income children is that they are acutely aware of the cost and the constraints it places upon their opportunities to participate in leisure activities. Where there are no concessions and no real awareness of the impact of even minimal costs, then low income children will suffer structural and social exclusion from the very few opportunities for play and association that exist.

CHAPTER 5

Friendships

C hildren and young people in rural communities have similar needs to their urban counterparts. They have the same need for opportunities to relate to other young people, to explore shared interests and to make and sustain friendships. Friendships can be vital for broadening horizons, developing self-esteem and for encouraging social skills and social interaction.

However, rural children are less likely to be able to meet and associate with a wide range of other children or experience different lifestyles. There is little cultural diversity in the countryside, with black children in particular facing very isolating experiences. The experiences of black people in rural areas has received little attention in the past, although since the report *Keep them in Birmingham* (Jay, 1992) was published, that gap has started to be addressed. In particular, the Rural Anti Racism Project, established within the National Council of Voluntary Organisations in 1996, is seeking to encourage good anti-racist practice within rural voluntary organisations.

What rural children tend to encounter is a very specific set of circumstances that can shape and constrain their ability to form and maintain friendships, particularly with children beyond their immediate environment.

VILLAGE CHILDREN

Children who live in villages may find it very difficult to meet other children beyond the confines of their village. Villages tend to have children of a wide range of ages who play together. Although in many ways this may be a rewarding experience, there can be problems through lack of choice and compatibility. The situation can also become intolerable as children get older and develop a strong desire for peer association, and also a need to form romantic attachments. Problems can also arise for children who are, for whatever reason, not included in village groups, leading to social isolation.

Dan explains that he lives in a small village where there are only seven children. Five are two years younger than him, and the other lives a long way out. He rarely sees any other children after school and he feels that the situation is getting worse for him as he gets older.

Where children have to travel to meet friends, they can find that there is little spontaneity as arrangements always have to be made in advance; there is not the casual and more informal structure whereby children just 'call' for one another. The need to be invited, and often transported, by adults can mean that parents have much greater power to control and influence friendships.

SCHOOL FRIENDSHIPS

Friendships made at school can be vital, particularly for children in small communities. However, due to the nature of many rural schools, particularly secondary schools with large, geographically-spread catchment areas, sustaining friendships after school can be problematic for some children. Respondents with access to private transport were most likely to be able to retain contact with friends after school. Respondents with access to two cars felt there were no difficulties in seeing friends after school.

Children who were not on a low income did not report many difficulties in maintaining friendships after school:

> [It's] *usually quite easy 'cos we get one of the parents to take us there.* (Dawn, aged 13)

> *I usually go over my friends' houses and sleep.* (Jenny, aged 12)

Where children did report problems, they tended to be associated with transportation and parental constraints of work and time:

> *I don't see very many* [friends] *on holidays and things. It's getting there 'cos mum works most holidays, dad's watching the racing and doesn't really want to take me.* (Scott, aged 13)

Fiona explains why she can't get to see her friend out of school:

Because she lives at [neighbouring village] – *my stepdad works so he's normally got the car when I come home from school.* (Fiona, aged 12)

FRIENDSHIP ON A LOW INCOME

The accounts below are from children and young people on a low income.

Low income respondents were much more likely to experience difficulties in seeing friends after school. Many low income children do not have access to private transport and, as with clubs and school activities, children were constrained by both cost and availability of transport. Many of these children expressed a desire to see their friends out of school, coupled with an awareness that this was not an option for them.

Stacey can't see her friends after school because of transport and the cost of petrol:

I don't play with them outside school. (Stacey, aged 12)

[You can't see friends] *if you ain't got the money to get the bus or your parents can't take you.* (Mary, aged 13)

Alison and Linda live in a small village on a low income. They attend a secondary school in a large town some distance from their home. They are unable to see friends after school because their mother cannot afford the petrol to take them. Alison says she is very aware of what her friends are doing together after school and feels very left out of things, especially when they are talking over what they did together the night before. Her family's house is already cramped and overcrowded and having friends to stay the night is not an option for her.

CONCLUSION

Whilst contact and interaction with other children is important for all young people, for children on a low income friendships can be particularly vital but problematic. Friendships can reduce the isolation felt from not being able to gain access to more structured activities, particularly those that cost money or require transport to take part in. The ability to make and sustain friendships can give an essential opportunity for social interaction. Unfortunately, because of the geographically-spread nature of rural communities, the need for transportation is again an important factor in determining ease of access. Lack of transport and financial considerations mean that children who suffer the dual impact of rurality and low income can face severe limitations on their capacity to maintain an adequate social life.

CHAPTER 6

Transport

A s we have seen, difficulty associated with transport and mobility is one of the factors most frequently associated with rural life. Public transport provision is invariably poor and scarcity and irregularity mean that ownership of private transportation becomes essential. Whilst problems of scarcity, timetabling and cost mean that the use of public transport tends to be fraught with complications, ownership of a car can also be problematic and many families struggle to keep what is, in effect, a lifeline giving them access to shops and facilities no longer available within their communities. Where families possess a car, if one partner uses it for work, the other partner and any children are left transport poor. Lack of private transport can mean heavy reliance on dwindling or nonexistent public transport, and can result in geographical and social isolation.

The majority of adults expect personal mobility as a matter of course and unless they are severely hampered by having no private transportation, they enjoy considerable freedom of access, both within and beyond their immediate surroundings. However, children in contrast experience very limited personal mobility and are heavily reliant on adults to supply their needs. This can be an area of dispute and struggle for autonomy and privacy.

THE ROLE OF TRANSPORT IN CHILDREN'S LIVES

In this part of the research, children were asked which forms of transport they had access to and how well it serviced their needs. Whilst bicycles were used by children as a recreational resource, they were not regarded by children to be a viable form of transport. Rural roads, which tend to be narrow, the lack of pavements and street lighting, and the distances between villages and settlements all militate against the bicycle being used as transport by children. Consequently, children focused on cars and public transport.

Of the 53 respondents who were not on a low income, 1 did not respond; of the remainder:

46 had access to a car; of these, 7 had two cars.
6 children did not have access to a car.

As was revealed when looking at opportunities for play and activities, transport to and from these events was often an essential component for participation. Children who had access to two cars were unaware of any difficulties that could arise in gaining access to events; transportation was not an issue for them. For children with access to only one car, there were signs that they could suffer limited mobility, especially if there was a parent at work using the car and they therefore had to resort to public transport:

The thing is, there aren't any buses – there's like one every hour and they don't fit in with the cinema times and you find that you either get there really early and you can't get a bus back, or it's the other way around. (Katie, aged 13)

Jane's father is at work and her mother cannot drive. She explained that this makes things difficult and sometimes costly:

There is nothing here for us to do so we have to pay to go places ... Sometimes dad gets annoyed about having to take me in the car so I end up walking. (Jane, aged 13)

Donna gave some indication that families may well be on a low income due to seasonal work and this affects their capacity to utilise their transport even though they have a car:

We're a bit tight on money at the moment, petrol's really expensive but we'll be all right in the summer 'cos my stepdad works at [local restaurant] *... so he'll get paid a bit more then.* (Donna, aged 12)

Rosie does not have access to a car. She explained how expensive it is for her family to go on the bus and how she can sometimes arrange a lift to go into town:

My mum can't get the money together 'cos there's four children ... sometimes I can't go but sometimes I ask my friend who lives in Exeter and comes down sometimes – he takes me in. (Rosie, aged 14)

OLDER CHILDREN

For older respondents, the issue of transport can be particularly acute. Older children have shown an urgent need to be able to reach beyond their own often small and constricting communities, and opportunities to meet with peers and experience a more stimulating and diverse social environment are seen as essential; transportation is a vital resource with which to meet those needs. Young people interviewed were very aware that access to private transport was vital and those who were able to drive were often running their own cars or sharing petrol costs with friends.

Privacy could also be compromised for some young people where there was a dependency on adults for lifts. Not all young people wanted their parents around when they were out socially and there were signs of conflict when adults knew details of where they were going and with whom:

You don't want to be seen with your parents. (Cathy, aged 14)

When my mum picks me up I'm like really nervous about what she's going to ask me. (Sally, aged 13)

Diana is 18 years old and has spent much of her life on a low income. She is now employed and has got her own car:

It's all changed since I've got my car ... It used to be very boring. [I] would go on walks, but the same old places. (Diana, aged 18)

Having a car has meant freedom and independence for Diana, who is now able to see her friends without difficulty.

TRANSPORT: THE EFFECT OF LOW INCOME

For children on a low income, once again a very different picture emerges with nearly 50% of low income respondents without access to a car. This compares to only 12% of non low income children not having access to a car.

Of the low income respondents, one did not reply, and of the remainder:

21 had access to a car; none had two cars.

20 children did not have access to a car.

Clearly, low income respondents were much more likely to have to resort to using public transport and to disproportionately suffer the difficulties that are contingent upon such usage.

Public transport in rural areas tends to be patchy, with considerable variability between areas. Difficulties encountered by these respondents included scarcity of provision and infrequency, with some villages having no bus service at all.

The following accounts are all from children and young people on a low income:

Sometimes you miss out on things badly ... I mean if I wanted to get somewhere really badly and like it was only until the evening ... and there was like only a bus in the day, I would go in the day and stay till the evening. But it's like there's not, some days like there's just not a bus. (Ella, aged 13)

Sometimes it's getting dark and raining and there's no buses and your parents are out and you don't want to hitch 'cos it's dark. (June, aged 15)

Young people can often find themselves involved in lengthy timetabling exercises as they try to work out opportunities to meet with friends or attend events. Ella explains how this and the cost of bus fares destroys any spontaneity and enjoyment she might have in trying to meet with her friends in the local town:

It's too expensive to get in, you've got to look at all the bus timetables and plan your day and I really hate doing that. I prefer just like to be able to mosey in and catch the bus in and just think, 'Oh well, the next bus is in a couple of minutes'. (Ella, aged 13)

Unlike their counterparts, low income children had a keen sense of the financial cost of both private and public transport.

[It costs] *quite a bit 'cos we haven't got a car – we have to get taxis down to do shopping and things and if mum wants to go out with dad they have to pay for a taxi to go out.* (Tara, aged 12)

It costs quite a lot 'cos my mum goes to [local town] *shopping so she has to have the bus fare there and back.* (Carla, aged 12)

It costs money to get out of [home village]. (Laura, aged 15)

I'd like to go to [local town] *sometimes. I used to but now I don't get my pocket money in my hand it's quite expensive to go from* [home village] *to* [local town], *it's like nearly £3 return. I don't really go – my friends do.* (Robert, aged 14)

Although she does have access to a car, Millie highlights the difficulties she faces living in a small village on a low income and reliant on her parents for transport:

There aren't any buses so we've got to go in the car if we go anywhere, which costs quite a bit in petrol ... We haven't got any shops so we've got to always pop down to the shop which is at [nearby village] *which is about three or four miles away. I have to rely on my dad all the time, which means if he doesn't want to or if he's doing something else, I can't go in.* (Millie, aged 14)

Transport problems were particularly acute for one large family living on a very low income in a small, isolated village. They owned a small, old car which they struggled to maintain as their only lifeline out of the village. It was generally used only once a week to go shopping. The children were not able to use it for access to clubs, activities or friends as there was no extra money for petrol:

It's very hard if I want to do something. (Linda, aged 15)

We take it in turns to go shopping with mum in town.
(Alison, aged 14)

For older children, the restrictions posed by cost and scarcity of provision could be intolerable and several of the girls talked of hitch-hiking as an alternative, if high risk, means of transport.

Of course, young people on a low income suffer the same possible problems with regard to privacy and autonomy as their more affluent counterparts and, where resources are scarce, there may well be greater scope for conflict with adults already under financial pressure:

She wants me to get the bus more but I'm not very together when it comes to that kind of thing, I just end up hassling my mum. (Paul, aged 14)

CONCLUSION

Although scarcity of public transport has been recognised as an important component of rural disadvantage, most recently in the *Rural White Paper*, what is rarely acknowledged is that the impact of inadequate provision will be disproportionately greater for some groups than others. Of these, children and young people are a group who already suffer limited mobility and a high dependence upon others for their transport needs.

What is apparent from the responses of children interviewed is that where families possess two cars, transport is not a critical issue. Where there is only one car, there are signs that some children are suffering when there are constraints on time and financial considerations. However, with 87% of respondents who are not on a low income having access to one or more cars, transport difficulties associated with the use of public transport, such as timetabling and the cost of fares, were not a significant issue. Conversely, low income children (with nearly 50% of these respondents without access to a car) reveal a high dependence on public transport and are correspondingly the most likely to suffer from the vagaries of scarcity and inadequate provision.

Although the provision of public transport in rural areas is often high on the agenda when consideration is given to rural disadvantage, what is revealed by this research is that provision alone is not the issue. The financial cost of using the service is often an important consideration on a low income and can easily result in an inability to utilise what little is available.

Furthermore, where low income families are struggling to maintain private transport, children are acutely aware of the cost of using it. In addition, there are indications that within families, access and mobility for children and young people may not be a high priority when there is an ongoing struggle to stretch already thin resources.

Whilst public perceptions of rural disadvantage often involve images of remote and isolated villages, children living in those villages with access to private transport and sufficient income may be well able to service their social needs. Paradoxically, children in less remote areas but on a low income may find themselves suffering from both physical and social isolation.

CHAPTER 7

Social space and relationships with adults

In many rural areas there is very little land that is not in private ownership. Farmland is decreasing and access to it for play and recreation may depend on the type of farming practised there and the generosity of the farmer concerned. Paradoxically, without access to farmland, villages are likely to possess very little public land and what little there is can be fiercely defended by adults.

Increasing numbers of affluent incomers and early retirers seeking a particular type of rural lifestyle can result in a powerful group whose interests may conflict with those of young people.

The exclusion of children and young people from influence and decision making can result in adult needs taking precedence over children's. Where there is a struggle for resources and space, adult needs tend to prevail and village halls, cricket pitches etc. can become adult preserves, off limits to children and young people. As a result, children can suffer from a lack of social space within their own communities.

One of the consequences of the lack of sanctioned space to play and congregate in is that children and young people become highly visible in their communities, and subject to adult scrutiny and in many cases disapproval. This can result in a situation whereby children and young people are seen as a problem rather than as contributory members of their communities. The concern about young people hanging around with apparently nothing to do is as much a phenomenon of urban areas as it is rural areas. However, in rural areas a small group of young people is very noticeable in an environment that has few community focal points and these young people are likely to be known by name by the adults who observe them.

Social space

In this section of the research, children talked about their home environments, where the good places to go were, and whether they felt at ease and welcome in their communities.

Many children felt that there were few places where they could go or that they considered to be good places to be in their towns or villages – a common response was that there was nowhere to go and nothing to do. The statement that there is nothing to do is almost the teenager's refrain. It can mean that there is nothing to do that particularly appeals at that moment in time. However, in rural areas it can be taken literally when the community boasts nothing more than a church and a bus stop. There may not even be a park to visit or a shop to congregate outside.

Even the presence of open fields does not mean there is somewhere for children and young people to explore. Modern farming practices involving heavy machinery and dangerous chemicals can mean that farmland can hold hidden dangers. Both farmers and private landowners can exert a jealous stranglehold over their land and in a society where there is very little land held in common, the reality for many of today's rural young people is that access to land can be contested or denied. This is apart from any restraints parents may place on their children from wandering off into unsupervised and unobserved locations:

> There aren't really any good places, we just play football and that. We used to use the fields at the bottom but since [local person] has bought it we haven't really got anywhere to go. (Jane, aged 13)

> There's nowhere really that you can go, there's nowhere that you can meet really. (Katie, aged 13)

> [We] can't be in mates' houses 'cos [parents] aren't going to let all your mates in the house are they. (Ella, aged 13)

> There isn't anywhere for us to like hang around, it's just like along the street, you walk down and back, there isn't anywhere for us to actually go. (Zoe, aged 12)

Fiona and Jenny sum up the boredom and frustration expressed by many of the respondents:

I don't think being young is very good when there's nothing you can do. If you're young and you live in a place where there's loads of things to do, I think that would be good, but I think if you live in [home village] *it's a bit boring. You just want to get out sometimes but there's nowhere to go so you're just stuck there getting bored.* (Fiona, aged 12)

Nowhere good to go, it's just a little village ... It's small, there isn't like a lot of people there and it's usually the older people who live there 'cos there isn't many young people. I'd just like to go somewhere where there's a lot more happening. (Jenny, aged 12)

VISIBILITY AND CONFLICT WITH ADULTS

One of the difficulties children face in their home communities is that they are frequently highly visible and this experience is compounded by a lack of facilities and social space.

Many of the places where children like to congregate can be particularly exposed in a small community where everyone knows everyone else. Where there is no space provided or sanctioned, hanging around the bus shelter or telephone box can expose children to censure and disapproval from adults, whose attitudes towards children, and especially teenagers, may be particularly harsh and are often informed by media representations portraying young people as threatening.

What was apparent from the responses was the high degree to which children felt observed and often censured and unwelcome. In this respect, both low income children and their better-off counterparts reported similar experiences of conflict with adults, and in many cases conflicting interests with older members of their communities, resulting in a lack of tolerance and what they perceive as a tendency to scapegoat young people.

Of the 95 respondents, 43% felt that adults minded children and young people being around or felt that young people were not made to feel welcome in their communities.

For respondents of 14 years and over, the figure rose to 60% reflecting the increasing antagonism that comes as children become young adults and are seen as more threatening. Whilst young children may be acceptable riding their bikes around the bus shelter, when teenagers do it, it is viewed in a very different light.

Young people showed a keen sense of injustice, particularly when they felt that they had very few opportunities to escape from the adult gaze and very little choice about where they were or what they could do:

> *Some people mind if you're just walking around or in the way in the shops – they get annoyed.* (Molly, aged 12)

> *They're forever moaning – I was riding my bike and the brakes squeak on it and this lady came out moaning at me that it was too much noise.* (Fiona, aged 12)

Feeling visible and unwelcome can be particularly difficult for children living in small villages where there are few places to hide and often nowhere to go. Both Dan and Gemma come from small villages:

> *Some people are OK but others get really annoyed at anything you do.* (Dan, aged 13)

> *They do get quite annoyed, they say kinda things like, 'Why don't you go and play somewhere else?'* (Gemma, aged 13)

One of the characteristics of rural areas is the large presence of the elderly and early retirers. Within the research area, in some locations such as Minehead the proportion of people classified as old age pensioners was 36% of the town's population. These groups have retired to the countryside, in many instances to experience a very particular type of lifestyle which will be orientated towards peace and quiet and can easily come into conflict with the very different needs of children and young people:

> *We're not allowed some places 'cos of the old people.* (Steve, aged 13)

> *Older people think that 'cos you're a kid you can be pushed around.* (Zoe, aged 12)

> *Most of the time it's like older people saying we're making too much noise and everything.* (Donna, aged 12)

> *They hate us, they see us hanging around the square and think*

we're causing trouble ... it's all old people [who] *phone the police all the time.* (June, aged 15)

In one community there were signs of conflict between children and adults around access to public space. Young people in a small tourist town had chosen to congregate in an area where there were shelters to sit in and some protection from the elements. In doing so, they came into conflict with both town authorities who felt they were affecting the tourist trade and adults in the town who perceived groups of young people congregating together as threatening. The resulting dispute was fuelled by local media reports and has left the young people with an acute sense of injustice and alienation:

> *There's been articles in the paper about like them being scared to go past and that but not many people mind, it's just like the old people get a bit worried.* (Debbie, aged 13)

> *Some people don't seem to like us being in the shelters, I don't know why, we don't shout at them or anything when they walk past.* (Mike, aged 17)

There were also signs of conflict between the needs of children and those of tourists. In certain areas, children were well aware of tourists and several young people felt that their needs were unlikely to be considered if they conflicted in any way with the perceived needs of tourists. The presence of tourists in some instances contributed to young people's feelings of dislocation from their communities:

> *If you walk through the town in the summer, all the holiday-makers are rushing past, and you sort of walk casually through them and they give you bad looks ... makes you feel you shouldn't be there.* (Molly, aged 12)

> *If you want to go to the youth club, there's these tourists here and they're staying for the weekend. They're always doing all the stuff that you want to do like using the pool table.* (Roger, aged 12)

POWER AND CHANGE

Children and young people were asked whether they thought they had the power to bring about change if they wanted to. Generally, they had little expectation of change and the overall experience was one of powerlessness. In many respects, this reflects children's structural exclusion from any forums of decision making and their lack of power to influence matters in which they have interests. Children showed a keen awareness that they would be neither asked nor listened to where their needs were concerned:

I don't reckon they'd listen to us. (Jenny, aged 12)

I don't know what you would have to do to try and get things. I don't think they'd really want to do it for so little children. (Scott, aged 13)

There's too many old people about and they wouldn't like it, I don't think. (Katie, aged 13)

By the time it got through the council you probably wouldn't want it anymore. (Tim, aged 12)

Zoe sums up some of the frustration several young people in her small town had expressed:

You ask council things and they don't really take much notice. They've come into school before and they say they'll do things and they never do. You just give up in the end ... They say, 'We'll see what we can do'. It seems that because we're kids they think we'll forget about it. (Zoe, aged 12)

When it came to children indicating what they would like to change, their needs tended to be very basic:

It would be better if the transport changed, and more set times of the buses and not so far apart. (Carla, aged 12)

I would like to make more places for the children to play ... bigger parks. (Sarah, aged 13)

I think they should make more transport 'cos catching buses is like really hard, they're really far apart ... and you have to wait ages to get back and they're too expensive. (Katie, aged 13)

[We] could do something in the village hall like a club or a disco

every fortnight 'cos there's nothing apart from car-boot sales.
(Maeve, aged 12)

LOW INCOME CHILDREN AND VISIBILITY

For children and young people on a low income, the issue of visibility can be particularly important. As the research has revealed, their opportunities for getting out beyond the confines of their villages and towns are severely reduced and they are correspondingly less able to escape from adult view. With nowhere to go and nowhere to hide, young people on a low income are more likely to be seen hanging around streets and bus shelters and can easily become known and labelled as troublemakers.

Conflict with adults can often escalate into conflict with the police and for young people in rural areas, police involvement can have a particular quality. Rural crime tends to be petty in nature but with an increasing population of affluent incomers, property and space can be zealously guarded from any perceived threat. High visibility can mean that certain children are at risk of scapegoating and can suffer from labelling by the police and other adults in their communities. This problem can be particularly acute for young people on a low income who may already be marginalised within their communities.

The following accounts are from low income children and young people, who highlight difficulties with the police and the impact this has on their lives:

If they think you are making any trouble they call the police ... all we're doing is playing ball and it doesn't say 'no ball games'.
(Ella, aged 13)

There's usually a PC ... walking around who has a go at anybody for virtually nothing. There's one group of us and if anything happens and they don't know who it is, they just blame it on me.
(Michelle, aged 15)

They're [the police] *always around – they do hold a grudge against us in* [home village] *– just 'cos of one or two people it's the whole lot of us, they're always out to try and get us all the time.* (Laura, aged 15)

If you have parties in anyone's house and the music's loud, you just expect the police to knock at the door any minute 'cos they always do. (June, aged 15)

We're out there and people are having a go at us as if it were our choice to stand out there in the freezing cold and the rain. If we had anywhere else to go we wouldn't be there, would we? (Cathy, aged 14)

PRIVACY

Heightened visibility can have the effect of denying young people any privacy to conduct their lives and pursue their interests. Again, low income children are the least able to have access to private space and have fewest opportunities to remove themselves from the adult gaze. For rural children, the visibility of living in a small community can mean that their actions, friendships and relationships are open to scrutiny by both family and community. This lack of privacy can create a particularly claustrophobic environment for young people and have repercussions for their ability to gain confidential access to services and advice.

Paula and Sally are both on a low income and they describe some of the problems they experience through lack of privacy, and the unfairness of getting known and labelled in a small community:

People in [home village] *aren't exactly the most pleasant of people. They're not private so if you tell someone a secret they tell everyone.* (Paula, aged 13)

Paula explains that she finds it difficult at her village youth club, which is the only provision available:

The lady what's there, we don't really get on together outside of youth club, then she holds it against me inside youth club – she lives just up the road.

She also highlights one of the problems associated with using a service like a rural chemist, which could have implications for young people seeking advice and medication, particularly if it is about contraception:

The only problem with the chemist in [home village] *is that there is one person who works there and lives in* [neighbouring village] *and she tells everyone the medication we've got.* (Paula, aged 13)

Sally lives in a small town where there is conflict over children and young people 'hanging around' in the shelters. She feels that young people have got a bad name and there is nothing they can do to change it:

I don't think we're welcome in the shelters ... nobody really listens to us, they just think we're a load of old junkies. Living in a place like this, everyone knows everyone else's business and like you know everyone but you can't keep anything to yourself.
(Sally, aged 13)

Lack of privacy and visibility is compounded by difference and people in rural communities have little first-hand exposure to other cultures and lifestyles. Consequently, they can be reactionary and prejudiced. Ella lives on a low income in a small rural town. She describes how as a young woman she suffers insults and labelling on the basis of her gender and racist abuse because of the colour of her skin:

They don't know me and they always call me slut and slattern, things like that and it's like you don't even know me, give me a break ... it's just people's attitudes and judging. (Ella, aged 13)

She explains why she doesn't tend to use one of the few facilities provided:

I don't like the people that hang around there ... going like 'niggers' and things like that. In London you're really unlikely to be a minority and like here I'm not very dark skinned but I get called 'Paki'.

Marginalisation and the fear of being seen as different is a very real concern for young people, and whilst adults can be harsh and critical, children themselves can also be particularly demanding. In rural communities, the scope for changing groups and meeting others of a like mind can be limited, therefore 'fitting in' can be essential. However, children on a low income can often have great difficulty keeping up with the styles and fashions expected by their peers and may find themselves teased and excluded:

> *The older people* [teenagers] *laugh at you 'cos of the way you are, 'cos if you're wearing something they don't like or think that is wrong they laugh at you.* (Sharon, aged 11)

Andrew is a young boy living with his mother in a small rural town. At eight years old he is already aware of feeling left out of things and the differences between his life and that of his friends:

> *I don't feel part of things but my friends do.* (Andrew, aged 8)

CONCLUSION

What is apparent from this section of the research is the high degree to which children felt observed and censured by adults. Whilst there will be children and young people who are able through sufficient income, or access to land, to fulfil their social needs within and beyond the confines of their village or town, for many others lack of social space means that they are inclined to hang around on corners, play in streets and colonise bus shelters. Whilst all these activities are not confined to rural children, what is particular about their experiences is the tight and often claustrophobic nature of village life, which means that everyone is intensely aware of everyone else and children are especially prone to scrutiny from adults who by right expect to have power and control over them. Where children generally are increasingly seen as threatening, rural children are no exception and teenagers particularly appear to be singled out for disapproval.

Children and young people also expressed feelings of powerlessness and some degree of dislocation from their communities. Whilst children and young people continue to be structurally excluded from consultation, decision making and allocation of resources, their needs will continue to be defined and determined by adult perceptions in forums that privilege adult interests.

For children and young people on a low income, lack of access to social space, heightened visibility and conflict with adults can have important repercussions for their sense of belonging. The interlocking effects of low income and rurality have a profound impact on children's ability to sustain themselves within small rural communities. Where rural communities suffer from inadequate resources and conflict arises around the use and allocation of social space, those on a low income have the least power to change the situation. As the research has shown, opportunities for children to meet their social needs beyond their immediate environment are severely reduced by the combined effects of inadequate transport, poor provision of services and financial constraints. As a result, low income children are more likely to be contained within their communities and suffer from increased visibility. This can be particularly difficult as children become older and are viewed with greater suspicion and less tolerance.

Heightened visibility can lead to increased opportunities for conflict with vigilant adults protecting their own interests, and may easily result in 'scapegoating' which escalates into involvement with police and authorities.

Whereas many young people feel a sense of separation from adults as they go through adolescence, for rural young people on a low income feelings of powerlessness, lack of privacy and a sense of injustice can easily lead to alienation, and these young people may find themselves isolated and marginalised.

CHAPTER 8

Conclusion

The main theme of this research has been the importance of listening to children and young people's voices and recognising that they are best placed to describe their lives and experiences. The clarity and perception that children bring to their accounts are in themselves a testament to children and young people's willingness to articulate and share their experiences, and are a powerful and refreshing antidote to the normative views of children's lives that tend to inform both public and policy-making discourse.

What has been particularly revealing and poignant are the voices of children and young people on a low income and the depth of difference and exclusion that they are experiencing. This is particularly important seen in the context of a research programme that did not seek to single out low income respondents in any way other than to note their income status. As a result, low income children were interviewed using the same format and questions as other respondents. However, their responses are a stark reminder of the impact of poverty on children's everyday lives.

SUMMARY OF MAIN FINDINGS AND RECOMMENDATIONS

Throughout the research, it has been apparent that rural living imposes a very particular set of circumstances upon children's lives, whilst also creating a particular social environment that can have implications throughout childhood.

RURAL IDYLL: MYTH OR REALITY

In chapter 2, children described what it means for them to live in the countryside, and what images and perceptions they have of town life.

Of course, children do not live in a cultural vacuum and public notions of the rural idyll can also have an effect on how children view their lives. For one group of children, these images were reflected in their accounts and they appeared to be experiencing many of the positive benefits of rural life; this was particularly true of younger children. However, for many of the other children, there were signs that all is not well in the countryside as difficulties with transport and limited access to facilities impinged upon their lives.

The significance of age was highlighted and an insight gained into the difficulties teenagers face as they reach an age when peer group association and the ability to maintain an independent social life are seen as crucial, and the lure of the town as a place of access and opportunities – real or imagined – is strong.

From children and young people on a low income, a very different picture of life in the countryside emerges, with many children express-ing feelings of isolation, boredom and a growing conflict with adults.

Greater support needs to be given to rural youth work, with an emphasis on providing affordable facilities for young people within their own communities.

Village and parish appraisals, where conducted, should actively involve children and young people in the process and in constructing plans of action.

PLAYING TOGETHER AND PLAYING APART

In chapters 3 and 4, children looked at the opportunities they felt were available to them for play and association, both within their towns and villages and at school. Here the overall impression was of a lack of provision generally, and signs that children and adults could be in competition and conflict in areas where resources and space are at a premium.

These chapters provide insight into the significant impact of rural factors such as problems of mobility, access, and scarcity of opportu-nity and resources upon children's lives. Although these factors are often implicated in rural disadvantage as it affects adults, there has been little knowledge or understanding of their effects upon children's social and cultural needs. Particularly revealing is the indication that these factors do not have the same impact on all rural children and that where there is sufficient affluence and mobility, localised lack of opportunity can be merely an inconvenience easily overcome. The burden of poor and inadequate provision falls most heavily on those with insufficient income and mobility to service their needs elsewhere. Of these children, those on a low income show clear indications of social and structural exclusion from the few opportunities that exist.

An important theme to emerge during the course of this research has been the cumulative impact of poverty and factors of rural disadvantage. Low income children showed an acute awareness of cost and its implications for their ability to participate, and the lack of concessionary places acts to reinforce their exclusion. Sadly, concessions can be in the front line when budget cuts need to be made. However, provision of concessions needs to be seen in the context of the very few opportunities that are available in rural areas and the value to these children of being able to participate and share in social activities with their peers.

Rural childcare initiatives supported by government funds should favour open access schemes or projects that offer financial concessions to families on low incomes.

Concessionary places should be provided as a matter of course when after-school activities and groups are established.

FINDING FRIENDS

Making friends and keeping friends can be a major preoccupation for children and friendships are vital for developing interpersonal and social skills. In chapter 5, children talked about their opportunities to make and maintain friendships and the particular constraints rurality can impose upon these relationships. Again, mobility was an important factor in access to friends, particularly due to the dispersal effect of children returning to their small communities after school. Again, income was a factor diminishing the effects of rurality for those with sufficient income and placing severe restrictions on children's social lives for those without.

GETTING THERE

Chapter 6 focused more closely on the theme of transport and highlighted some of the difficulties that emerged in earlier chapters. Most children and young people suffer from limited mobility and reliance on adults and this can be exacerbated in a rural environment where access to clubs, friends, facilities etc. can mean travelling considerable distances.

Having access to private transport can be crucial, particularly where public transport is scarce and inadequate. A disturbing gap is revealed in this chapter between those children on sufficient income, of whom 87% had access to one or more cars, and those on a low income of whom nearly 50% did not. This highlights the high dependence of low income respondents on public transport. Their responses revealed that it was not just the vagaries of provision that created difficulties, but also an inability to pay where provision was costly. Clearly, more research is required in this area where improved provision alone is often seen as a policy response to rural transport problems.

Transport needs analysis in rural areas should focus on the needs of children and young people, and on affordability of public transport as much as availability.

Greater financial concessions should be made to families on low incomes who use public transport, for example, reduced rate weekly passes.

BEING SEEN BUT NOT HEARD

Whilst previous chapters focused on the impact of rurality on children's access to opportunities for play and association, chapter 7 explored children and young people's social relations within their rural communities, and the struggles that can arise in trying to gain access to social space.

What emerges is the high degree to which children and young people feel observed, and in many cases censured, by adults in their communities. Visibility in small communities is compounded by a lack of social space and feelings of powerlessness. The influx of wealthy incomers and early retirers can constitute a powerful group with particular interests and images of the countryside to defend. Where there is a struggle over scarce resources and space, decisions about allocation and possession are made in forums that exclude children and favour adult needs. Teenagers felt particularly singled out for disapproval and intolerance.

The issue of visibility is seen to be especially acute for children and young people on a low income who already suffer from severely reduced opportunities to escape the confines of their villages and towns and are correspondingly contained and highly visible within their communities. Conflict with adults and the elderly can easily escalate into conflict with the police and low income young people are particularly exposed to the risk of scapegoating and labelling by police and adults.

This chapter highlights the need for more tolerance and understanding of children's needs in rural communities. As long as children and young people are seen as a problem and there is little willingness to embrace them as valued members of the community, their sense of exclusion and alienation will persist.

District and parish councils should consult with children and young people over planning issues, particularly when they involve building on ground that children may use as unofficial play space.

Children should be consulted in any housing need surveys in villages.

Rural communities through the Church, parish council and youth service should liaise with children and young people over the designation and protection of recognised play space.

Consideration should be given to how churches and other public buildings can be made more available and child friendly so that they can be used by children and young people as a legitimate focal point.

THE NEED FOR FURTHER RESEARCH

Throughout this research, The Children's Society has been particularly concerned that children and young people are given the opportunity to speak for themselves. In this we have been rewarded by the forthright and revealing way in which they have responded.

Clearly, there is an important need for more research into how children and young people experience their lives in order to gain an understanding of their needs, desires and aspirations. This is especially true of rural areas where the focus has tended to be on 'hard' statistical data. This does nothing to aid understanding of life as a lived experience and, through the dominance of 'urban' models of need, is manifestly inadequate as a measure of rural poverty, obscuring as much as it reveals and raising important questions of how we understand poverty in the countryside, and how we measure and reveal it.

Whilst experiential data is invaluable for insight and understanding, it is important to ensure that children and young people are not encouraged to speak into a void, that their views and experiences are respected and supported, and that where issues of importance to children and young people arise, their voices can be heard.

Most recommendations for action in this conclusion relate to local responses rather than national ones. This is because children experience exclusion at a local level and some simple actions can reduce this experience. Although some actions such as providing financial concessions require local authorities to spend money, others such as consulting with children and young people over planning issues do not.

There is a need, however, for the government to recognise the particular needs of children and young people when considering rural issues. More specifically, there is a need for government-backed research into the lifestyles and needs of rural children on a low income. The debate about what constitutes a low income will continue but the focus on the impact of living on a low income has to be raised beyond the area concepts of deprivation.

The most important finding of this research has been the fact that most children and young people on a low income in rural areas have a qualitatively different experience of rural life than their better-off counterparts. Children have produced evidence of both structural and social exclusion and a picture for many of life on the margins of their society. Insight gained into the interlocking and cumulative effects of rurality and low income raises questions about the nature of social exclusion within small communities, and the impact of poverty on rural lifestyles already affected by factors associated with rural disadvantage.

If rural children on a low income are to experience an improved change in lifestyle and remain as a vibrant part of rural communities, then their very existence and prevailing needs have to be recognised.

References

Alcock, P. (1993) *Understanding Poverty*. MacMillan.

Archbishop's Commission on Rural Areas (1990) *Faith in the Countryside*. ACORA Publishing.

Archbishop's Commission on Urban Priority Areas (1985) *Faith in the City: A Call for Action by Church and Nation*. Church House Publishing.

Cloke, P., Edwards, G. (1986) 'Rurality in England and Wales 1981: A Replication of the 1971 Index.' *Regional Studies*, vol. 20.4, pp. 289–306.

Cloke, P., Milbourne, P. (1994a) 'Households Containing Young Persons Aged Under 16 Years'. *Lifestyles in Rural England Briefing Report*. Rural Development Commission.

Cloke, P., Milbourne, P., Thomas, C. (1994b) *Lifestyles in Rural England*. Rural Development Commission.

Cloke, P., Milbourne, P., Thomas, C. (1995) 'Poverty in the Countryside: Out of Sight and Out of Mind'. C. Philo (ed.) *Off the Map*. Child Poverty Action Group.

Department of the Environment/Ministry of Agriculture, Fisheries and Food (1995) *Rural England: A Nation Committed to a Living Countryside*. HMSO.

Department of Social Security (1995) *Social Security Statistics*.

Derounian, J. G. (1993) *Another Country: Real Life Beyond Rose Cottage*. National Council for Voluntary Organisations.

Duke of Westminster (1995) *Equality of Opportunity for Rural Children: Country Children Count*. ACC Publications.